Lerner SPORTS

SPORTS ALL-STARS

KATIE LEDECKY

Jon M. Fishman

Lerner Publications ◆ Minneapolis

Lerner Publications Company
An imprint of Lerner Publishing Group, Inc.
241 First Avenue North
Minneapolis, MN 55401 USA

For reading levels and more information, look up this title at www.lernerbooks.com.

Main body text set in Albany Std 22. Typeface provided by Agfa.

Editor: Rebecca Higgins **Designer:** Susan Fienhage **Photo Editor:** Brianna Kaiser

Library of Congress Cataloging-in-Publication Data

Names: Fishman, Jon M., author.
Title: Katie Ledecky / Jon M. Fishman.
Description: Minneapolis : Lerner Publications, [2021] | Series: Sports all-stars (Lerner sports) | Includes bibliographical references and index. | Audience: Ages 7–11 | Audience: Grades K–1 | Summary: "Superstar swimmer Katie Ledecky has six Olympic medals and fifteen World Championship medals. Watch this Olympian as she continues to make history"— Provided by publisher.
Identifiers: LCCN 2019045729 (print) | LCCN 2019045730 (ebook) | ISBN 9781541597501 (library binding) | ISBN 9781728400990 (ebook)
Subjects: LCSH: Ledecky, Katie, 1997—Juvenile literature. | Women swimmers—United States—Biography—Juvenile literature. | Swimmers—United States—Biography—Juvenile literature. | Women Olympic athletes—United States—Biography—Juvenile literature. | Olympic athletes—United States—Biography—Juvenile literature.
Classification: LCC GV838.L43 .F57 2021 (print) | LCC GV838.L43 (ebook) | DDC 797.2/1092 [B]—dc23

LC record available at https://lccn.loc.gov/2019045729
LC ebook record available at https://lccn.loc.gov/2019045730

Manufactured in the United States of America
1-47854-48294-3/16/2020

CONTENTS

WORLD'S BEST

Katie Ledecky leads the pack in 2019.

In July 2019, for the first time in six years, US swimmer Katie Ledecky lost. She was competing at the swimming world championships in Gwangju, South Korea. She had won the 400-meter **freestyle** race every year

- **Date of birth:** March 17, 1997
- **Position:** swimmer
- **League:** international swimming
- **Professional highlights:** won a gold medal at the age of 15 at the 2012 Olympic Games; won four gold medals and one silver medal at the 2016 Olympic Games; works with TYR swimwear to help sell swimming gear
- **Personal highlights:** grew up in Bethesda, Maryland, near Washington, DC; loves chocolate milk; was named one of *Time* magazine's 100 most influential people in 2016

Ledecky (*center*) and teammates watch the final 50 meters of the 4x200-meter relay.

since 2013. But in Gwangju, she finished in second place. Then she withdrew from the 200-meter and 1,500-meter races.

Ledecky was sick. She didn't feel like eating and wasn't sleeping well. Tests at a hospital confirmed she had a **virus**. She spent two days resting before helping the United States finish second in the 4x200-meter freestyle **relay**.

The next day, Ledecky competed in the 800-meter freestyle. It was her last race and chance for gold in the world championships. But she still wasn't back to full strength. "I had to dig really deep," Ledecky said. "I did not feel very good when I dove in the water."

Midway through the race, Ledecky held the lead. But she was passed by Simona Quadarella. Quadarella held a one-second lead with 200 meters to go. In the 400-meter freestyle a few days earlier, Ledecky's illness had caused her to slow down near the end of the race. But this time, she had the strength to go faster.

Ledecky swam the final 50 meters more than two seconds faster than Quadarella and won the race. She was thrilled to win another world championship gold medal. "It's special to be able to pull out a swim like that and just trust that I could do it," she said.

Ledecky (center) takes gold in the 800-meter freestyle.

SWIMMING AND WINNING

Washington, DC, is the nation's capital.

Katie Ledecky was born on March 17, 1997, in Washington, DC. She grew up in nearby Bethesda, Maryland, with her older brother, Michael, and their parents, Mary Gen and Dave Ledecky.

Mary Gen Ledecky passed her love of swimming to her kids.

Mary Gen was one of seven children who all learned to swim at an early age. From 1975 to 1978, she was a member of the University of New Mexico swim team. When Michael was nine and Katie was six, Mary Gen enrolled them in swimming lessons at Palisades Swim & Tennis Club in Cabin John, Maryland. They joined the Palisades Porpoises summer swim team.

At Palisades, Katie swam in races with her friends.

Katie and Michael liked swimming so much that they signed up to swim all year at Palisades. Katie played other sports too. But an accident in fourth-grade gym class made her rethink the sports she wanted to play. During a basketball game, she slipped on a wet spot on the floor. She fell and broke her arm. “That’s kind of when I started thinking, ‘I really like swimming. I’m going to not risk playing other sports,’” she said.

Katie was a fast swimmer, and she pushed herself to go faster. She began training with swim coach Yuri Suguiyama at the Curl-Burke Swim Club. She joined Suguiyama's **elite** group of swimmers.

In August 2011, Katie was ready for her first big **meet**. She swam in four events at the US junior national championships. She won three of them. Katie was one of the top young swimmers in the United States.

Katie celebrates winning the 800-meter freestyle in the 2012 US Olympic Team Trials.

Katie kept increasing her speed. At junior nationals, she won the 800-meter freestyle in 8 minutes and 39 seconds. Almost one year later, she competed in the same race at the US Olympic Team Trials. This time, she won the race in 8 minutes and 19 seconds.

The victory at team trials showed Katie's commitment to improving. It also meant she would compete at the 2012 Olympic Games in London, England. The high school freshman would face the world's best swimmers on the sport's biggest stage.

The United States sent 529 athletes to London to compete in the 2012 Olympic Games. Katie, at 15, was the youngest person on the team.

"JUST GO FAST"

Ledecky dives into a pool during a swimming class. She teaches young athletes to swim faster.

At the highest levels of swimming, races are often won by hundredths of seconds. To give herself the best chance to win, Ledecky always pushes herself to swim just a bit faster than the race before. Her desire to go faster and faster began with the Palisades Porpoises.

Ledecky practices during the 2016 US Olympic Team Training Camp.

As a six-year-old swimmer at Palisades pool, she wrote time goals on slips of paper. Then she tried to swim fast enough to reach the goals. She still sets time goals for herself, and she doesn't make them easy to reach. "I try to set goals that seem kind of unreasonable at first," she said. "As I work toward them, the more reasonable they look."

To reach her goals, Ledecky works out six days a week. She begins her training days at about 4:00 a.m. After she has a breakfast of peanut butter toast and a banana, Mary Gen or Dave drives her to the pool. Ledecky swims about 4 miles (6.4 km) in 90 minutes.

After the morning swim, Mary Gen picks her up at 7:00 a.m. In the car, Ledecky drinks chocolate milk and eats an omelet with bacon, cheese, and tomatoes. She has eaten so many of the omelets that the restaurant that makes them, Ize's, calls them Katie's Gold Medal Omelet.

Omelets provide the fuel Ledecky needs to recover from her workouts.

Ledecky often naps in the morning and then eats lunch. She likes chicken and salads with avocado. Later, she might have a snack of fruit, peanut butter toast, or yogurt. Then it's back to the pool from 3:30 to 6:00 for a 5-mile (8 km) swim.

Three days a week, Ledecky also does **dryland training**. She does exercises such as **planks** to strengthen and stretch her muscles. Stronger muscles don't tire out as quickly during races.

Planks strengthen the whole body.

Ledecky and Simone Manuel attend a swimming award show.

Ledecky prepares for months for big races. On the day of the meet, she tries to stay loose and have fun. One way she does that is by goofing around with her fellow swimmers, including good friend Simone Manuel. “We dance together, we sing together, and I think it just kind of keeps her relaxed and reminds her to just have fun—no pressure, you’re a good swimmer, just go fast,” Manuel said.

FAME AND FORTUNE

Ledecky signs autographs in 2019.

Ledecky often wears TYR swimwear during her meets.

Ledecky stays focused on the pool and her workouts, but swimming is just part of her life as an international swimming superstar. In 2018, she agreed to work with TYR swimwear. The company agreed to pay Ledecky $7 million for her help selling swim gear until the end of the 2024 Olympic Games in Paris, France.

When Ledecky was about 12 years old, she discovered the benefits of chocolate milk. It has **protein** and other healthful ingredients she needs after workouts. And, of course, it tastes delicious. She began packing a bottle of chocolate milk in her bag along with an ice pack to keep it cool to drink after swim meets and practices.

As an adult, Ledecky still loves the sweet drink. She's part of the Built with Chocolate Milk campaign. Ledecky and other famous athletes spread the word about the benefits of chocolate milk and encourage people to drink it after workouts.

Ledecky refuels with chocolate milk after tough workouts.

Community Helper

Ledecky has been giving back to her community since she was a teenager. Her desire to help people is as strong as her drive to win races. As a high school student, she volunteered with Shepherd's Table. The group provides food and services to people without homes. She also worked with Bikes for the World, building bikes for people who needed them.

As an adult, Ledecky spends time with the Wounded Warrior Project. She meets wounded soldiers, takes photos with them, and signs autographs. She also works with Catholic Charities to improve people's health, housing, and much more.

Shepherd's Table serves meals to people experiencing homelessness.

Ledecky answers questions during a 2018 press conference.

Ledecky's fame has grown quickly since making the 2012 US Olympic team. In 2016, *Time* magazine named her one of the 100 most influential people in the world. She has appeared on many magazine covers, including the July 2018 edition of *National Geographic*. She was the first female Olympic athlete to ever appear on the magazine's cover.

Time magazine reports on current events in the US and around the world.

GOALS

Ledecky sprints during the 800-meter freestyle.

Some swimming experts didn't expect Ledecky to win the 800-meter freestyle at the 2012 Olympics. Everyone knew she was talented, but the event was her first international race.

They thought the 15-year-old would come up short against the world's best swimmers.

Ledecky took the lead early in the race, and no one could catch her. She finished four seconds ahead of the second-place swimmer and won the gold medal. Her time of 8 minutes and 14 seconds was the second fastest ever.

Ledecky holds up her gold medal in 2012.

In 2016, Ledecky swam in her second Olympic Games, in Rio de Janeiro, Brazil. In London, she had competed

Ledecky poses with her five medals from the 2016 Olympic Games.

in just one race. But four years later, she was ready to take on the world in five races. She won four of them. Ledecky took gold in the 200-meter, 400-meter, and 800-meter freestyle races. She also helped Team USA win the 4x200-meter freestyle relay and finish second in the 4x100-meter relay. It was one of the greatest Olympic swimming performances ever.

Ledecky continues to make new goals for herself and work toward fulfilling them. She has her eyes set on the 2020 Olympic Games in Tokyo, Japan. She'll be the huge favorite to win every event she enters. But Tokyo won't be the end of her swimming journey. "I see myself still swimming for many years to come," she said. "It's something I really love and want to continue doing as long as I can, as long as I'm having fun with it."

Ledecky plans to keep crushing her goals.

All-Star Stats

Ledecky, fellow US swimmer Michael Phelps, and US gymnast Simone Biles dominated the 2016 Olympic Games. Take a look at where they ranked in medals won compared to other athletes who won big in London:

Athlete	Country	Total Medals Won
Michael Phelps	United States	6
Katie Ledecky	United States	5
Simone Biles	United States	5
Katinka Hosszu	Hungary	4
Simone Manuel	United States	4
Maya DiRado	United States	4
Nathan Adrian	United States	4
Emma McKeon	Australia	4
Penelope Oleksiak	Canada	4

Glossary

dryland training: a swimmer's workout done on land instead of in a pool

elite: the best of a class

freestyle: a name for a race in which swimmers can use any swimming stroke

meet: a gathering in which swimmers race one another

planks: balancing on the toes and forearms while holding the rest of the body above the ground

protein: a substance in all living plant and animal cells

relay: an event in which teams take turns swimming

virus: a tiny organism that can cause disease in humans, animals, and plants

Source Notes

6 Maggie Ryan, "How Katie Ledecky Overcame Illness and Surged from Behind to Win at the World Championships," PopSugar, August 14, 2019, https://www.popsugar.com/fitness/Katie-Ledecky-Wins-800m-at-2019-World-Championships-46488638.

7 Karen Crouse, "Katie Ledecky Rallies for Gold in 800 Free at World Championships," *New York Times*, July 27, 2019, https://www.nytimes.com/2019/07/27/sports/katie-ledecky-swimming-world-championships.html.

10 Philip Hersh, "Chasing Katie Ledecky," ESPN, August 4, 2016, http://www.espn.com/espn/feature/story/_/page/espnw-ledecky160804/what-makes-olympic-swimmer-katie-ledecky-remarkable.

14 Hersh.

17 Hersh.

27 Christine Brennan, "Katie Ledecky's Historic Sponsorship Deal Signals Intent to Swim through 2024," *USA Today*, June 8, 2018, https://www.usatoday.com/story/sports/christinebrennan/2018/06/08/olympics-katie-ledeckys-historic-deal-signals-intent-swim-through-2024/685042002/.

Further Information

Derr, Aaron. *Individual Sports of the Summer Games*. Egremont, MA: Red Chair, 2020.

Fishman, Jon M. *Michael Phelps*. Minneapolis: Lerner Publications, 2017.

Hellebuyck, Adam. *Olympics*. Ann Arbor, MI: Cherry Lake, 2019.

Katie Ledecky—Olympic Swimming
https://www.olympic.org/katie-ledecky

Sports Illustrated Kids—Olympics
https://www.sikids.com/olympics

Team USA—Katie Ledecky
https://www.teamusa.org/usa-swimming/athletes
/Katie-Ledecky

Index

Photo Acknowledgments

Image credits: Catherine Ivill/Getty Images, p. 4; Oli Scarff/AFP/Getty Images, p. 6; Maddie Meyer/Getty Images, pp. 7, 19; Orhan Cam/Shutterstock.com, p. 8; Nicholas Hunt/Getty Images, p. 9; Monkey Business Images/Shutterstock.com, p. 10; Frederic J. Brown/AFP/Getty Images, p. 11; Jl Jl Press/AFP/Getty Images, p. 13; Ronald Martinez/Getty Images, p. 14; koss13/Shutterstock.com, p. 15; TORWAISTUDIO/Shutterstock.com, p. 16; Kevork Djansezian/Getty Images, p. 17; Yong Teck Lim/Getty Images, p. 18; Theeradech Sanin/Shutterstock.com, p. 20; Chris Seward/Raleigh News & Observer/Tribune News Service/Getty Images, p. 21; Toni L. Sandys/The Washington Post/Getty Images, p. 22; Brian Ach/Getty Images, p. 23; Al Bello/Getty Images, p. 24; Popperfoto/Getty Images, p. 25; Harry How/Getty Images, p. 26; Clive Rose/Getty Images, p. 27.

Cover: Maddie Meyer/Getty Images.